NUNderwear

Tales of Catholic School
Survival in the 1960's

Alice F. Pauser

First edition

ISBN 978-0-578-28996-0

Printed by: BooksOnDemand.com
Cover Layout and Design: Tia Fulmer, BooksOnDemand.com

SCRIPTED
CHAOS

Post Office Box 258173, Madison, WI 53725

www.scriptedchaos4u.com

Illustration by a survivor

Table of Contents

Introduction

As a child I was always much smaller than the rest of the kids, but I was fierce and an old soul. In the early 1960's, and within the first year of Catholic school, I was organizing a band of covert guerilla operatives to protect us from the "Brides of Christ."

This is my satirical perspective from pain, a fuzzy memory, and humor.

Dedication

For my grandmother, Frieda Alice, who was the guiding light in my life, welcomed and encouraged my rebellious nature, and made my childhood tolerable.

Nun's habits in the 1960's was one of the most recognizable types of religious uniforms. They typically consisted of a white headpiece, black veil, a black loose tunic that reached the ground, and had long wide sleeves. There was a crucifix necklace or rosary that hung from a cord belt, black hosiery, a pair of simple black shoes, and rulers.

In the beginning …

There were the rules.

- Do not swing high on the swings and tuck your skirt between your legs
- Only slide down the slide with your skirt tucked between our legs.
- No using the monkey bars when boys were near in case they looked up our skirts
- Get money for the church
- No playing with the boys
- No passing notes
- No being alone with a boy
- No standing next to a boy in the choir. We were in front, and the boys were in back.
- Get money for the church
- No sitting next to boys at lunch
- No slouching while you're kneeling
- No fidgeting
- No eye contact when you were getting punished
- No humming during class
- Get money for the church
- No complaining about cleaning the votive candle area
- Act like a lady
- Submit to God without question
- Submit to the teachers without question
- Get money for the church

The Catalyst

I didn't want to go to school in a uniform. I wanted to wear tennis shoes and shorts and the little flowered headscarf my grandmother made me. I wanted to go down to the creek and poke dog poop with a stick and wipe it on the neighbor boys' bicycle tires.

Not a uniform with a white shirt, tie, knee socks, and itchy plaid skirt.

My mother took me the first day. I stood in the doorway of that classroom and thought, "Now what?"

Three months in I understood that this was not going to be a good place for any of us. Every time they let us out for recess, I ran the three blocks home.

I saw things. Even at six years old, I knew these things weren't right. Every morning we'd have to sing a hymn that was broadcast over the intercom. Something about "Suffer the Little Children Unto Me."

Literally.

So, it became clear to me.

I declared war.

I learned how to survive there through seventh grade, though it was often creative and not without consequences.

Who was Sister C.?

⁓⁓⁓

"We had to wear those wool plaid skirts.
It took me a long time to figure out why I
was terrified, yet oddly aroused,
by men in kilts when I was an adult." A.

She wasn't the principal, but she was always in the church office. If we ever got sent to the office with something to drop off or pick up, she was there. Sister C rarely spoke to us. Her breath smelled of strange mouthwash.

Maybe there was a reason she didn't leave the church office. In retrospect, she was probably too drunk to make it up the stairs.

In all fairness to her, we were the reason she drank, but that woman could play the piano like she learned it in a gin joint.

Learning the Alphabet

In those days, you learned the alphabet in first grade. I didn't like it and the kid sitting next to me was a much better student than I was, but he was obnoxious. He had that alphabet thing down to a tee. Sr. M always called on him. He was her favorite and as a result heard a lot of "teacher's pet" yelled in his direction by the other boys. Later in the year, they threw him out of a bus window into a snowbank.

I had been looking at pictures in the Bible and there was this spectacular scene of Romans in a sword fight. We had to draw little pictures by the letters, so I put "K" is for kill and had a soldier on his back with a sword stuck in him and blood spraying out. My parents were called and told I wasn't acting an appropriate manner with my behavior and illustrations.

If they only knew what was coming.

School Supplies

Every year we would get the list of school supplies needed for class.

My favorite thing was crayons. I remember the year I got my first box with the built-in sharpener. It was a rite of passage. No more crayons the size of my grandfather's cigars.

The rubber erasers were always a must because they could be used as a weapon that didn't leave a mark.

There was a boy in the class who managed to get a piece of eraser stuck in his nose. As I recall, another kid had dared him to poke the pencil up there.

The nun told him his mother was coming and he would have to go to the doctor. When she asked him who told him to do that, he didn't tell on anyone.

The other kid outed himself by yelling, "It's a miracle!"

For some kids, their butts would become the shape of the chair in the principal's office.

Staring Death in the Face

❧

"If there ever was a moment
that I feared for my life,
it was giving a nun
"that look" of defiance" M.

In second grade, our class was split up and some of us were assigned to Mrs. S. and the rest to Sister P.J.

P.J. was a linebacker in nun's garb who used that huge rosary on her belt as a weapon, almost like nunchucks. She blocked the sun coming down the hallways and I highly suspected she wore steel toed boots. She was particularly abusive with the boys, slapping them or grabbing them out of chairs, and would slap that pointer stick on the blackboard so hard that it vibrated. I dreaded going into her classroom for any reason because I knew my covert warfare might not work on her, and my name, too, would be listed among the martyrs.

I was assigned to Mrs. S. She was mean, with a bra so pointed it could impale you, and wore high heels that clicked on the floor when she walked. At least we could hear her coming. Halfway through the year, she was killed in a horrific car accident. I overheard my parents say she was decapitated. We were forced by the school to go to the funeral home in a neighboring town. It had an old wood heater in the viewing area. The nuns walked us right up to the casket. Mrs. S. had her blue suit on with a scarf tightly tied around her neck. She looked like she had been dipped in wax. Later, one of the girls said, "Do you think they put her head back on like Frankenstein?" To which another girl replied, "No, because you would have seen the bolts."

I had nightmares for months.

First Confession

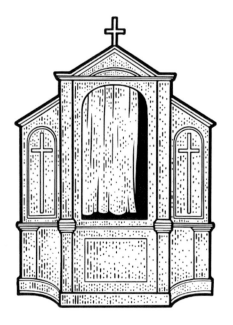

In second grade, getting ready to make our first confession, we were all trying to figure out what we could offer for sins. (Because seven-year-old children really don't have many sins for which they need to atone.) So, I thought, I'd been mean to my sister, disrespected my parents, and told a lie about candy. The heavy-duty stuff. Well, according to the student grapevine, a classmate asked his older brother what he should say, and he told him to say, "I have touched myself in an impure manner." It was a fiasco; the poor kid was yanked out of the confessional by the priest who was supposed to be absolving him.

I figured out if I moved my knee on the kneeler a certain way, I could make the indicator light that someone was in there flash like Morse code. That, and if I crouched down enough, when the priest would slide the window open, he wouldn't see me and close it again and then I'd pop back up. I would always get three Hail Mary's, two Glory Be's, and told to say the Act of Contrition.

Like that ever happened.

First Holy Communion

Illustration by a survivor

White dress, shoes, socks, veil, rosary, and prayer book. Entire families in the pews watching the procession. We had supposedly reached the "Age of Reason" and were on that freight train heading down the Sacraments. The one Sacrament I had trouble with was Holy Orders because I thought that is what we were getting every day from the nuns. We also received a scapular, which was a sign of piety. (Two saint images held together by strings so that one was in the front and one in the back.) But who is pious and penitent at seven-years-old? I could barely get my mind off the fact I accidentally walked in on my parents in a moment of en flagrante delicto.

Communion hosts tasted awful and they either stuck to your tongue or the roof of your mouth. And God pity you if you ever got caught taking it out of your mouth. One of the boys thought if you dipped it in the holy water fount it would soften it up. Not a wise move. He wound up cleaning erasers for the rest of the year.

The Clickerati

"When I realized that we said the same
prayers repeatedly, it was a type of brainwashing.
It was also why I never named my children
Jesus, Mary, or Joseph." D.

One nun had a clicker and trained us to all genuflect at the same time when she snapped it. We'd file into church, she'd click it, and we'd all go down. One of the boys took a clicker out of her desk and when the students were going up for communion, he clicked it, and everyone obeyed the command. But then he started doing it rapidly and it looked like we were having seizures. When he was ferreted out, he left the church by his hair.

To this day I cannot go to a dog show where trainers use clickers without getting a twitch in my leg.

Third and Fourth Grade

I am sorry for my sins.

I am sorry for my sins.

I am sorry for my sins.

I am not sorry for my sins.

I am sorry for my sins.

I am sorry for my sins.

I am sorry for my sins.

I am not sorry for my sins.

By this time, we were honing our skills into fine tools. Some classes were combined, and we had a lay teacher named Mrs. K. She was wonderful, and I looked forward to seeing her every day. That was until I became the scourge of the class, and I was innocent this time.

We had a German priest visiting and were putting on a skit for him. My paternal grandmother who was German and despised the Catholic Church taught me a song to sing for him. Well, part of it translated to something like "My dog went past with pickles on his ass." I wrote on that blackboard "I am sorry for my sins" about a hundred times.

The Boston Terrier Effect

Illustration by a survivor

My younger sister was an incredibly quiet, kind child who was put in a class where the nun was an abuser. Physically and mentally. My sister would cry on the way home and hold my hand. I told my friend, "I want to do something." So, I took the crayon box out of the nun's desk and went over to the rectory, where the priest's Boston Terrier was out in the yard. I emptied the crayon box out and scooped up a big turd in the box and put it back in her desk drawer. Unfortunately, when she came in the next morning, she blamed one of the kids for pooping in their chair.

When it was discovered none of the kids had pooped in their chair and that it was coming from her desk drawer, the classroom was evacuated.

We had spies everywhere who would report to us.

The Tie Dye Effect

⚜

"I just dreaded getting up in front of the class for those spelling bees. If you spelled the word wrong the nun would yell, "SIT DOWN!" You felt awful and humiliated. That is why I am accountant, so I do not have to spell, just work with numbers." E.

A substitute teacher came in whenever our regular teacher had a medical procedure, and that substitute sucked the joy out of all of us. All the wonderful things we had with our former teacher were erased like they didn't matter. I had my hands welted because I was left-handed, and she wanted me to write with my right hand. The boy who sat next to me came up with a genius plot. He thought we could bring squirt guns with bleach in them. We knew exactly what it did because our parents bleached everything. We decided that every time she walked up the row between the chairs, we would spritz the back of her habit.

But in the end, we feared we would get caught and that St. Jude, the patron saint of impossible cases, wouldn't have our backs. We stuck with fake coughing and knocking our pencils off the desk.

Lunch Ladies and Their Domain

"Whatever it was they put in those leftover
sandwiches from lunch and fed us for an afternoon
snack was suspicious. I had a vision John the Baptist's
head was on the desk next to me and said,
"Do not worry, it only hurts for a minute." F.

Tyrants with long, heavy metal spoons and hairnets. White uniforms, aprons, and sensible shoes. The kitchen boss was a big woman with stray hairs on her chin and a bellowing voice. We would get our trays and form a line and she would yell if the line wasn't straight. We had to say thank you for everything put on our plates, including the rutabagas that were disguised as carrot sticks. I now imagine the ladies sitting out back on overturned buckets, hairnets askew, smoking cigarettes and mumbling "I wish we could poison all those little monsters."

One girl sitting at the table with us did not have any food because she accidently broke one of the many terrifying saint statues when she was dusting in the classroom. However, Sr. L made her sit with us and watch the rest of us eat. Some kids whose parents could not afford tuition were treated like slave labor to 'earn' their lunch. I put my jelly sandwich in a napkin to give to her and when I was found out, I was locked in the dark coat room for over an hour. I moved toward the door, where a thin line of light ran across the bottom.

I don't know what my father said to the nun, but I was never put in the coat room again.

The Menstruation Contemplation

In fifth grade, the girls were taken into a classroom with a film projector. One of the lay teachers announced we were going to watch a "feminine hygiene" movie. What the hell? There was Sister MT sitting way in the back like she was about to see a horror film.

The projector made its weird whirring sound and a perfectly coiffed woman appeared and said, "Girls, today we are going to talk about a very personal and private subject: Menstruation." We all looked at each other and shrugged. It went downhill from there. The film showed the Kotex pads and the Kotex belt positioned on a mannequin. We were told you can't go swimming and you shouldn't wear light colored or tight-fitting pants or light-colored skirts and to not make it a topic of conversation. The moment she said that it immediately became a topic of conversation. By the end I felt like everything about menstruation was shameful, dirty, and needed to be hidden.

The first girl who got her period in our group was revered by us as a sort of holy virgin mystery.

The Glamorization of the Christ Child

Illustration by a survivor

Christmas was always a time of chaos and festivity at the school. We all displayed our holy cards like a poker hand on the cafeteria tables. Many had an angel hovering over the shoulder of the Virgin Mary with the look of complete and utter confusion. Perhaps thinking, "What exactly is it I am watching for?" And we'd trade them. "Hey! I'll trade you that John the Baptist for the one that got eaten by lions." We had mini plastic stable scenes to hang on the trees and all the ornaments we made were strictly religious. I thought dinosaurs would add a nice touch.

The life-size manger scene was always placed in the same spot in the church. To the right of the main altar at the top of three stairs. There were so many votive lights around it that you almost had to wear sunglasses if you were seated in the front pew. We all knew the drill. File past the manger, kneel on that rock-hard stair, and kiss the Baby Jesus' feet. If you had elderly members in your family, the ushers would have to help them off the floor, which held up the line and made people angry because, after all, they had to get downstairs for coffee and a cigarette.

Then came the idea. We, as in the small group of us that were always in trouble, talked about how we could make it better. I suggested painting the Baby Jesus' toenails. So, I borrowed my mother's brightest red bottle of polish, which she NEVER wore to church because it was Satan's color. Two of the other kids stood lookout while I glammed up his Lord, Jesus Christ.

After somebody told on us, I was in the car with my dad and he said with a heavy sigh, "Why is it that they never even suspect anyone else?"

NUNderwear

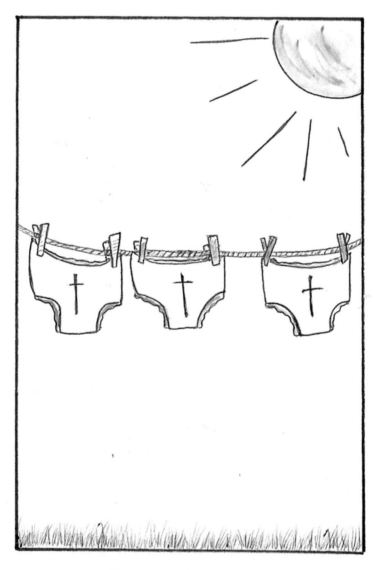

Illustration by a survivor

The backyard of the convent was walled off so that you could not see what was going on. We were told it was for privacy, so we could not see the nun's underwear hanging out on the clothesline. We could see everyone else's underwear in the neighborhood but not theirs.

Of course, we wanted to get a look over that fence. One day after school two boys decided to boost a third one up to get a look. They were too successful, and the kid fell over into the nun's yard.

The rumor was the family moved but it was without the kid because nobody ever found him.

Obviously, no one understood that telling a kid not to do something in Catholic grade school was a direct challenge.

The Basketball Revelation

Illustration by a survivor

Once during sixth grade, we were standing around watching the boys play basketball. We were not allowed to stand too close. I am sure it would have made us fallen women in the making.

Sr. L. was out there, too. She was a lanky, quick moving juggernaut that could slap the hell out of you before you even saw her coming.

The game was moving along when WHAM! a ball hit her in the head, knocking off her veil. Everyone froze. First, because we could not believe she had hair and second because she did not even flinch. You know how when a firework explodes, and the flares are in every direction? That is how we ran. Indiscriminately, fast, intent on escaping.

They managed to herd us together and get us back into the school. What was interesting is none of the kids I was with were laughing, just giving each other darting glances.

We did, however, know we had leverage because we saw her hair, which was almost like seeing her naked.

The Humiliation of R

"Catholic school screwed me up for life.
I am only attracted to large women who wear
black and hit me with rulers." G.

Early in my school career we had a boy who wet himself because the nun would not let him go to the bathroom. She made him stand in front of the class to humiliate him. Many of the other kids started crying. I told everyone I knew what had happened. This boys' father, who was a big man, came to the school the following day. There was yelling, and R. was taken out of school and was placed in the forbidden land of public school.

How does a child process any of this?

The "Publickers"

And they call us the "Catlickers." I was told not to go over to their playground and not to go in the school. But I did. It was like deliberately defying God.

And we decided to play with each other, ride bikes and did fun stuff in the neighborhood. I have no idea why this was such an awful thing. Some of our parents were not happy we were sneaking around with the enemy. I only understood why they were upset with us going over to one house, where they made booze in the basement, and it was rumored that the grandma had been a 'saloon girl.'

One kid had a 'mixed' family, meaning one Catholic and one Protestant parent. The mom would come to church on Sunday with the kids. We did not know where the dad went. Probably into the mouth of hell.

By the time sixth grade rolled around I was openly and flagrantly going over to girl scout meetings at the Lutheran church. Man, those Lutherans kicked our asses at cookie sales.

When the Baptist minister and his family moved into the house next to us, my mother sprinkled holy water around the edges of our yard.

The Room with
The Holy Stuff

Right outside of the church worship area, there was a small room that had holy items for sale. Statues, little creche scenes, rosaries, holy cards, and holy water in little bottles, which I found out later did absolutely nothing for you if you drank them.

I was always fascinated by the objects. I once bought a holy card with the image of St. Frances Cabrini, the saint of immigrants. On the card, she was seated in a chair, wearing black, flowing robes, with a bow tied at her chin to keep her veil in place. Her hands were gently folded in her lap, and her expression was kind and peaceful. I loved her. She was everything I thought a saint should be because she was reputed to kind and was loved by the community she served. I still have her card.

There were dozens of holy cards available. It was hard to choose. I just wished some of them were not saints tied to pillars with arrows stuck in them, impaling Satan, or their heads on a chopping block.

When the nuns told us we should aspire to be like the saints, I always thought, "You first."

What was going on

in the Rectory?

Who knew? The only time I was ever in there was in the front office with my parents, getting yelled at for misbehaving or refusing to say my prayers.

The housekeeper was a widow or an old maid. I do not know which. There was always a rumor that "something was going on" between her and the priest. What was going on? Card games, wine drinking, French maid's costumes? It was a huge mystery.

Fr. T smoked cigars. He would sit out in the back of the rectory with his cigar and the newspaper. It was the only time I thought of him as a regular guy.

The rectory looked to me like a bastion of torture, where you would go in and never come out. I never trick or treated there.

I did, however, steal something from the rectory. It went into my shoebox reliquary and was used as an accoutrement for my doll house. No other doll house in the world had a miniature framed image of the Infant of Prague.

What happened to
Mrs. A?
A Huge Scandal.

She was often seen going into the rectory. In my sixth-grade year, she ran off with Fr. H, got married, had a baby, and they lived happily ever after, even though they were both excommunicated from the church.

The Votive Conflagration

Illustration by a survivor

Sometimes the girls would be put into the church to help clean it. I never once saw a boy dusting the pews or polishing around the altar.

There was something fascinating about the votive lights. They were in racks. The small ones in front for little prayers, the blue medium ones for regular sinners and in the top row with the big red votives with the candles that burned for about a week for the people who were in real trouble. The racks were in front of the Mary and Joseph statues. One was set off to the side, as well, for sins that had yet to be categorized. There was a little metal box at the lower part of the rack to pay for your candle. When I put in my coin, it often made a hollow sound, and I worried no one was paying.

One day we thought it would be magnificent to light all of them. Not because we wanted to do it as a prank; we thought it would be a way to send a big prayer.

It did do something. Three nuns had to frantically snuff out about sixty candles while trying not to catch on fire.

The Convent Liquor Deliveries

bottles

It was common knowledge that some nuns could throw back a few cocktails. We heard the stories when the grown-ups gathered. One of the boy's older brothers found out there were regular liquor deliveries to the convent. The boys knew the deliveries were put inside the porch door.

A well-timed plan made it possible for them to steal one of them. I do not know how they divided it up or if they threw a party.

I do know that the one of the sixteen-year-old boys was sent to special camp for a few months. When he came back, he smoked cigarettes and had a tattoo, and every girl in town wanted to marry him.

The Lie about Love thy Neighbor

ReAl FRIENDS ♡

Illustration by a survivor

The church was supposed to be welcoming, generous, and kind but there was a huge layer of hypocrisy. Even though the school took in children of poverty, those children were not always treated well.

We (the kids) were always trying to help. We told our parents and some of them stepped up to the plate with food, money, and clothing.

I remember there was a family that had old wood plank floors in their house. The girl in my class had head lice on more than one occasion and owned about two pairs of socks and one pair of shoes. The nun called her stupid and dirty. A small group of girls befriended her. We were all told to not touch her because we would catch lice. We did it anyway.

My mother was not a fan of my asking to go home on the bus with the girl. She finally gave in and provided me with some things to take with me.

That experience is burned into my memory. I was so overwhelmed. When I got into the house it smelled like wood smoke, it was stark and dimly lit.

I looked down at the table and there was a church envelope that you put your Sunday donation in. They had nothing and yet they were sent those envelopes and expected to give.

When my mother picked me up, I was questioning why some people must give money to the church. Why wasn't the church giving them money and food? Why weren't they taking care of them?

The answer I received set in stone my defiance against the church. Some people are meant to suffer, I was told. It was God's will.

I Was Never Asked to Be the Virgin Mary in a Play

The number of skits or plays we were forced to be in was staggering. The kids that got the best spots had parents who were subordinate to the nuns and priests. I remember one mother who scrubbed the floors of the convent, did their laundry, and a whole list of other things that ensured her daughter would never get punished like some of the rest of us. Even though my parents were generous with tithing, this never spared me the corner or the bench in the office.

Then one Christmas, I got to be the narrator of the play despite my previous behavior. I was a fluent reader, which is probably how I got the gig. I was excited and so were my parents. Even my grandmother, the radical German Lutheran, came.

There came the part when Jesus was born, and they were supposed wrap him in swaddling clothes and lay him in the manger. But somebody didn't put the right size blanket in the manger, so Baby J wasn't fully covered. "Mary" started to cry, the three wise men walked off, and I said, "Can we just go now?" I looked over at my grandmother and she winked.

We all went down to the cafeteria for a reception. We always had good receptions with great food and women in elaborate aprons serving it. It happened that our Bishop was visiting for a few days. He was an arrogant, condescending person who was in office until I graduated from high school. His assistant followed him around like a capuchin monkey on a leash.

When you approached the Bishop, he extended his creepy gloved hand and you were expected to kiss his ring. That evening I said to him. "I like your gloves. My aunt wears some just like that."

Purchasing a Pagan Baby

IS AWARDED TO

Alice Petlock

St. Anthony of Padua School

Park Falls, Wisconsin

In Testimony of an Offering made to the
Pontifical Association of the Holy Childhood
for the *Adoption of a PAGAN BABY*
who will receive the Name of

CHRISTINE MARIE

in *Holy Baptism*

FOR THE ASSOCIATION

NATIONAL DIRECTOR

Rev. Raymond Schoone

DIOCESAN DIRECTOR

DATE March 1, 1966

There was a little pastel booklet that talked about 'purchasing' a Pagan baby for $5 and you could name it and it would be baptized. I believe this was the first scam I was ever exposed to. Where were these babies?

On my way to school one morning, I found a five-dollar bill on the sidewalk. I thought it was miracle and a sign that God wanted me to get one of the babies. I asked my mother and she said yes. She filled out the form with me and I proudly brought it to school, and I named the baby Christine Marie.

I never even received a picture of the baby I purchased. Where exactly did those five dollars go? My guess is right into the rectory's pocket.

The Church Picnic

Every summer there was a church picnic and we all looked forward to it. There was a cake walk. The music started, and we all marched around the chairs. Then Mrs. H stopped the music, and the scramble began, leaving one boy out. It was the wrong boy to leave out. He was an ornery kid who shoved another boy off a chair. That's all it took, and the fight began. Hitting, rolling around, yelling. The smaller boy pushed the other one, who tripped and fell backwards, hitting his head on a chair and splitting it open. Blood everywhere, girls screaming, and parents running like a herd of buffalo toward the melee. About two hours later the kid came back with his dad, he was sporting several stitches. It was the greatest picnic, ever.

What Fresh Hell is This?
It's Arts and Crafts

Illustration by a survivor

Throughout year there was always some horror of an art project going on.

Here are two that come to mind.

The Popsicle Stick Crucifix

We had to glue together popsicle sticks in the shape of a cross and then glue an image of Jesus on it from some drawing we would trace and cut out. To top it off, the rosary was made of raisins for beads and string. The dog loved it.

The Plastic Bottle Depiction of the Assumption of Mary

The old Palmolive dish soap bottles that were translucent white or blue were turned into religious masterpieces. We soaked them to get the labels off, then cut a rounded opening in the side so you could peer into the bottle. We were given cotton balls to glue to the bottom like clouds and then glued sparkly holy cards of Mary rising to the sky to the back of the bottle. We also sprinkled glitter on the cotton balls. Sort of like a diorama. I think this was the beginning of people putting statues of Mary in a half-buried bathtub in their front yard.

When I came home with my bottle, my grandmother happened to be taking care of us while our parents were out of town, and she asked me, "What do you want to do with it?" We silently walked to the burn barrel near the alley, and I threw it in.

What's in the Janitor's Closet?

Illustration by a survivor

It was always locked. Our school janitor was a kind man and I liked him. Anyone who sprinkled sweeping compound on the puke of a terrified student was a hero in my book.

Why is it when there is a locked door you immediately want to know what's inside?

One day the door was left open, and we snuck in. It smelled awful from all the chemicals, but there was toilet paper. Lots of toilet paper. We took some and ran, feeling the exhilaration of a heist.

We got outside behind the school and stopped. One of the boys said, "What are we going to do with this?" Not knowing the answer, we took it all back and put it in the closet. As we were coming out, the janitor saw us. He never said a word. We loved him even more.

"I remember the smell of the sweeping compound
the janitor used in the hallways. It was overpowering
and to this day if I smell anything like it,
I get anxiety ridden." R.

The Mighty Censer

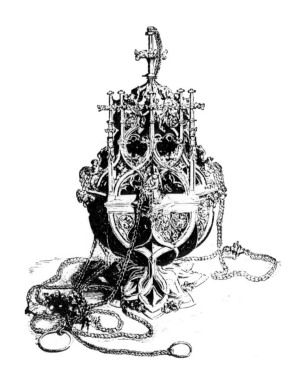

The Easter season was the worst for me.

Our classrooms were filled with all the preparations to get us through as devoted little children of the church.

First, there was Lent, and I had to give up something as penitence. Every year it was agony. What could I do without for forty days? Candy, movies, my favorite TV show, or watching the neighbor boy through my dad's binoculars? How about I give up Lent? So, one year it was candy. My grandmother decided that there was a way to get around it. She made maple syrup candy and she put it on our oatmeal., telling my mother "It's maple syrup, not candy." She was a genius.

We also couldn't eat meat on Friday and had to fast before Sunday Mass. I thought I was going to perish.

Ash Wednesday meant we had to go up and have the priest smudge our forehead, saying, "From dust you came and to dust you shall return." And we were told to never touch the ashes. Everything was so positive.

Then came Palm Sunday and my sister and I would whip each other with the palms on the walk home, yelling things like, "Jesus is coming to town, get off the sidewalk so he can get through."

But the worst was Good Friday, the censer with the burning incense, the stations of the cross, the long service. What kid wants that?

The incense made a lot of people cough and feel ill, but the priest just kept going up and down the aisles, swinging that thing back and forth.

Easter Sunday eventually arrived and there were baskets of candy from the Easter bunny (a purely Pagan image), a joyous Mass, and a great dinner.

Once, my grandmother said after a few martinis, "Why does everything in the Catholic church have to be such a goddamn ordeal?"

To me, that was one of the greatest statements in my parochial school career.

The Forbidden Sacristy

"I became very sexually active and had risky
behavior after attending Catholic school. In fact,
it was a way for me to rebel against the church.
That, and it was the 1970's." C.

No girls allowed. Only priests and altar boys. I was even told by my mother to not go in there.

It seemed strange to me that the only reason the "Altar Ladies" could go in there was to clean, take the altar linens to be washed, and do other housekeeping. So ladies were good enough to be maids but not to take part.

The One Moment I Thought I would Make a Good Nun

In fourth grade, I found a book about all the orders of nuns. It was fascinating and talked about how they developed, what countries, types of monastic living, and lengths of rulers.

There was one order that had the coolest outfits. They looked like the flying nun. I decided to go to the rectory and talk about it. I brought the book with me and showed it to the priest. He was very kind about it and did not laugh in my face or tell me I wouldn't be a good nun. He said one sentence. "Alice, you know that if you want to belong to this order of nuns you have to take a vow of silence, don't you?"

I did not let the door hit me in the ass on the way out.

The Guy in
the Back Pew

Illustration by a survivor

When I was about 12 years old, I started noticing an older boy who always sat in the back of the church. My heart fluttered whenever I saw him. I used to pretend we would get married and wrote his name about a hundred times in my diary. I stopped putting my hair in a ponytail so I would look more 'mature.'

My mother would grab my arm on the way out of church and said, "Stop staring at him!"

I suppose my thoughts were breaking the commandment, "Thou shalt not covet the last pew."

The "Cover-Up"

"They were trying to kill us.
That is why I became a
weapon's designer in college." J.

There was a sign in a glass case at the top of the entrance stairs to the church that spelled out the "dress code." My classmates and I were reminded of this every time we were getting dressed for Mass.

Part of it referred to the women dressing "modestly."

No sleeveless dresses or low-cut tops. Modest length skirts, chapel caps, or veils.

The only rules for the men were take your hat off and keep your family under control during the sermon.

I hated my chapel cap. My mother would secure it with a bobby pin, and it would poke my head. One Sunday, I decided to fold it like a paper airplane and attach it myself.

It wasn't well-received.

Let's Have a Bake Sale

One of the good memories I have of Catholic school was the bake sales. The altar society and PTA would do this on a regular basis.

Breads, cookies, cakes, pies, and cinnamon rolls.

There was an old, heavy-set woman with a thick Hungarian accent who was the best baker of them all. I was always excited to see what she'd bring. There were always a lot of people at her table.

Sadly, even the church ladies could be petty. I remember one saying to my mother, "We thought she was a Jew when she first came here."

I had no idea what she was talking about. But I was taught Jesus was a Jew and if his mother baked like that, we were good.

The Pregnant Sister Dilemma

One of the fifth-grade girl's sisters got pregnant in high school and the gossip was vicious. I think "Love thy neighbor" was brought to a screeching halt. The family was virtually ostracized.

We had no clue how she got pregnant, but we had all kinds of wild theories. Was it an angel? Did she sit too close to a boy on a park bench? Had she rode around in a boy's car?

We were pretty sure a boy had something to do with it.

One day she disappeared. People said she went to her "aunt's house." In fact, she was sent to an unwed mother's home run by nuns in Minnesota.

She eventually came back, and it was weird.

One of the girls in my class was having a birthday party and my other classmate, the sister of the pregnant girl, was not invited. I said to my mother, "I do not want to go if she's not going."

My mother said, "Fine" and the three of us went to see my grandmother, the Lutheran hellraiser. I overheard them talking in the kitchen.

My beautiful, no nonsense, rebel of a grandmother said, "People can be hypocrites no matter what church they go to."

The family of the pregnant girl moved that summer. I looked up hypocrites in the dictionary.

That's when I immediately understood the saying, "If the shoe fits, wear it."

Report Cards

How my parents dreaded them.

There was one that spelled it out clearly.

It was an additional report titled "Growth in Desirable Habits and Attitudes".

A check mark meant improvement is needed.

Here is how mine went:

- ✓ Conforms to school regulations
- ✓ Is courteous in speech and manner
- ✓ Respects church property
- ✓ Is reverent at prayer and in church
- ✓ Keeps desk and materials neat
- ✓ Keeps profitably busy
- ✓ Obeys promptly and willingly

Apparently, I did do well in the category of exhibiting mental happiness. Really?

That Old Nun that Came to Visit

She came to visit in the Spring of 1965. She was old! I mean almost set in stone.

The other nuns took turns bringing her to each of the classrooms to listen to songs and skits. The woman smiled all the time. At everything. Even in the lunchroom.

We suspected her hearing was bad.

We found out that in fact she heard every single word.

When she was being helped out of the room, she turned and waived her cane at us yelling, "You devils!"

Our pride carried us through rest of the day.

Terrifying
Tether Ball

In elementary school, it was all about avoiding tether ball. Who thought up that game? It's as bad as dodgeball.

Kids got aggressive and if you ever showed a sign of weakness, that ball would knock you flat out.

There was an older girl who enjoyed slamming that ball on the younger kids and then laughing. Now that I think of it, she was the size of an adult. My mother always said she was probably "held back."

I Wore
Saddle Shoes

I wore saddle shoes almost every day. I had a brown pair and a black pair. To me, they were ugly.

When I asked my mother why I couldn't have pretty shoes, she responded, "They have to go with your uniform."

I was informed that "flashy" shoes were disrespectful because we needed to be humble in our appearance.

It was confusing because our Sunday shoes were "flashy." Shiny, with buckles and little cut-outs.

I tried several times to sneak out of the house with my Sunday shoes on, but it never worked. I'd get twenty steps from the house and my mother was on me like a wet blanket.

I did, however, sneak one of her Kotex belts out of the house. The other kids found that way more interesting than fancy shoes.

Poem to Jesus ...

Oh Jesus,

I am trying to be good,

Like a pious child should.

I do not want to be a sinner,

I want to be a winner.

I will pray every day and be good in every way.

It was my first smoke screen in writing.

The Epic
Book Report Fail

Occasionally, we had to do a book report.

My younger sister and I loved reading. We spent hours poring over our Encyclopedia Britannica and the dictionary, where we would read a word and one of us would guess what it meant.

I found the story of the Goddess Athena. Wow! She was amazing, so I did the report on her heroic powers as the goddess of war.

Apparently, I had committed blasphemy, according to the commandment "Thou shalt not have any gods before me." My response was, "She's a Goddess, not a god." This did me no favors.

My sister and I built a little hidden altar to Athena in our mom's peony garden. I was a proud Pagan even then.

The Blasphemous Pajama Parties

Pajama parties served a dual purpose. The first was to be silly and the second was to mock our school. What could possibly go wrong with a bunch of pre-teen girls running unfettered through the house, fueled by sugar and adrenalin?

The conversations were so inspiring, and we fed off each other

The "remember when" ones were the best.

"Remember when Sister A told us to be little Christian soldiers and we started marching and she yelled at us?"

"Remember when [that boy] kept staring at me? He's so cute and I think he likes me."

"Remember when your sister told us nuns never had to pee and that's why they never went in the girl's bathroom?"

"Remember when I looked up sex in the dictionary in the back of the room and circled it and Sister P wanted to know who the sinner was that did it and somebody asked, 'What does sex mean?' and she left the room and brought the principal back?"

"Remember when she hit [a boy] in the back of the head with a book and we rubbed jelly sandwiches on her chair?"

Then somebody's mom or dad would yell from upstairs: "Girls, if you don't settle down everyone is going home." Our goal was to make them so mad they'd yell "Jesus Christ!"

That Odd Priest from Some Other Parish

There was a priest from another parish who would visit a few times a year. I never felt comfortable around him. He would drop in and sit in the back of the classroom, taking notes on a small pad of paper. His floor-length outfit was different from our priests, adorned with too many symbols, like Holy Ghost crucifixes and chalices, and black buttons. Sort of ominous. I remember Fr. T coming down the hall at a rapid pace with his cassock just whipping around. But this priest was slow and deliberate, almost silent in his movements, like a spy or the harbinger of death.

He did, however, provide us with some amusement. He had a terrible singing voice and when he would sing in parts of the mass, we would start giggling and kicking the legs of the kid sitting next to us.

I told my grandmother he said "Kyrie Eleison," I know I mispronounced it because my grandmother asked me why the priest was talking about Jackie Gleason.

Seventh Grade Apocalypse

I didn't hate all my time in Catholic school -- only about ninety-nine percent. It was the rigid structure and the punishments that had me rebelling every chance I could.

Some kids went through it unscathed, and others were horrifically abused. As for those people that say this never happened in Catholic schools in this country, I cast thee out.

When I look back on all of it, I do not regret any of my disruptive behavior.

In Catholic school, I developed a very dangerous sense of humor as well as the ability to spot brainwashing from a mile off.

In seventh grade, my time as a parochial school student ended when my parents agreed to send me to public school. I decided to tell the nuns myself that I wasn't coming back instead of waiting for my parents to tell the school.

I had friends in public school that were rooting for me to run as fast as I could to get out of there. My dad asked, "Who told you to tell Sr. C that you weren't coming back?" I answered, "EVERYBODY!" Meaning everybody that said I would like it at the other school.

The funny thing is, no one at St. Anthony's protested my leaving or tried to change my parent's minds. In the end, I threw myself into the arms of junior high.

I think my parents hoped I would be less prone to getting in trouble in public school.

My Civics' teacher in junior high turned out to be a jerk. He used to take his shoes off and walk around in his stocking feet. One day he told me I didn't act like a lady and obviously my parents had no control over me, and later that day I threw his shoes down the trash chute. But that's a story for another day.

Later in Life ...

When my daughter was born my grandmother said, "Do not name her Chloe because that's the name of a 'loose' French maid in a romance novel I read, and do not send her to Catholic school."